Playerbook

for any number of players using any means

Jason Thomas

DEATH-SPIRAL 10, 1

PASADENA CA 2024

ISBN 979-8-218-98945-3

Notes on *Playerbook*

The pieces in *Playerbook* belong to a genre I call *subject music*—a term I began using roughly twenty years ago to describe pieces that share certain practical aspects and artistic objectives. From a practical standpoint, a piece of subject music is created by indicating a desired perceptual result. This differs from many traditional scores that tell us what to do, not what sound should result. I began utilizing this approach not so much to achieve a desired sound (although this is often the case) but because traditional notation often privileges aspects of sound which are at best peripheral to my aesthetic concerns. (For instance, few of my own works use specific pitch or standard rhythm as organizing principles.)

A major correlation also exists between a focus on physical production and presentation (media and venue, etc.) and an expected physical response in the listener. One frequently hears of edge-of-seat and "goosebumps" responses to music, in much the same way that comedy, suspense, and erotic films are geared to evoke an emotional response in the viewer. Since this is not my priority as a composer, I have focused instead on developing a creative process that is, in a sense, exempt from such expectations.

Initially, I composed standalone pieces indicating perceptual results via text or, in some cases, alternate notation. Looking back, I can see that the implications of these pieces were not fully grasped. Take for example my early piece *for six players*—must that necessarily be the case? Were I to write the same piece today, I would likely indicate that while the six sounding parts *may* be realized by six players, a smaller number of players might just as well satisfy all six parts, as could a computer playback in deferred time or any other suitable means. Other pieces are similarly burdened by the equivalent view of an early car as a horseless carriage, where features relevant to the animal no longer apply to the machine.

Following these standalone works, I completed *Immaterial* in 2004, a collection of 100 compositions for imagination only. Stemming from this work, the question naturally arises as to why *any* piece of subject music would be performed, rather than simply imagined. *Immaterial* closely encapsulates the genre of subject music, and also contains the first written description of the term (outside of notes to an earlier conference presentation), resembling the summary above. One reader went so far as to misunderstand subject music as music for which a physical realization is not required. While this is certainly possible with much subject music, it is not exclusively the case, just as imaginary music (of which there are many examples by others, several predating my own) need not be subject music—for instance, imaginary pieces which make reference to existing sounds in the physical world.

Since all subject music is by default created with an awareness of perception, it must be understood that imagining sound is entirely different from sound perceived through external stimulation. Certain works may best be served by the former and others, the latter, in part based on the degree to which features particular to either mode of realization are advantageous or disadvantageous. Some pieces could certainly be realized just as well via physical performance as by imagination. A small number of pieces in *Immaterial* or *Playerbook* could even appear in the other volume without being entirely out of place.

The pieces in *Playerbook* do not specify the means of sound production, nor do I care to exploit any particular instrument or technology for theatrical purposes, etc., in their realization. For me, the decision to opt for physical performance over imagination rests primarily on the extent to which I would prefer that the perceiver be free to let their mind wander while listening to a given piece, rather than being exclusively focused on its formal development. Externally perceived sound affords the listener greater leeway to place certain aspects of the work (or the entire work) into the background, whereas this is less likely to happen when every aspect of a piece is strictly imagined—fundamentally, a more intentional process.

It should be noted that pieces on either side of this decision fall along a continuum, occupying a wide and interesting middle ground. One piece in *Immaterial* asks the perceiver to vary their focus between two simultaneously perceived sounds. This is something we do frequently in music perceived with the ears, either consciously, when we decide to focus on a particular aspect of the music, or subconsciously, when nudged by the music itself, such as when a repetitive part recedes while simultaneous contrasting material is introduced. In the process of writing these pieces, I have grown both fascinated with our capacity to place our focus where we wish, and intrigued—and occasionally frustrated—by the out-of-the-box defaults we are hardwired to impose as humans, which will continue to bear on my music (and that of any other composer), regardless of our intent.

Once designated for physical performance and not imagination, works which specify a desired perceptual result but leave open the means of realizing it may well complicate the role of those called upon to play them. A great deal of interpretive freedom is implied, which naturally begs the question of what means and manner of approach best supports a given work—and no less crucially, what approaches may ultimately work to its detriment by emphasizing performance concerns at best only tangentially relevant.

The simple answer is that a performance of subject music may use any means suited to achieving the indicated perceptual result. Those aspects not indicated in the score are left to the discretion of those realizing the work, with the general condition that those areas left unspecified are of lesser importance—by no means a blank canvas for performers to exploit at the expense of the clarity of those aspects which *are* specified.

In the notes for *Immaterial*, I reflect on some of the difficulties computer music poses for the composer. While one can feasibly control every parameter of a given sound, this can lead one farther into the weeds, as merely ignoring or delegating certain less crucial aspects of a piece often becomes impossible. I find this position analogous to a playwright who is given complete control over the staging of a play, and must now *also* decide aspects of tangential relevance to the drama, such as costumes, lighting, and the like—all complicated technical facets of production which one *could* indicate in the script, but which are more typically delegated to specialists in those areas.

This analogy is all the more interesting given the recent trend toward experimental productions that restage well-known theatrical works in unusual or provocative settings. A work of Shakespeare or Euripides might now be updated to take place during the Vietnam War, or in a contemporary corporate boardroom—creating not only a visual tension or dissonance but an altered lens through which the work is understood. When this is done successfully rather than gratuitously, the work takes on a new perspective, without sacrificing the clarity of its structure and meaning. In general, this approach is more suited to familiar works, since we are better able to appreciate a new frame around a work we already know.

Unlike the works in *Immaterial*, which all begin with a direction to "imagine" a particular sonic description, I could have chosen from a few different ways to begin the pieces in *Playerbook*. The term "play," my ultimate choice, was not the obvious winner from the beginning. Generic alternatives such as "produce," "cause to sound," "realize," "cause to be perceived," etc., proved too cumbersome or awkward. I considered these unwieldy descriptions because "play" can easily evoke an aspect of traditional performance, whereas I only wish to indicate that the pieces are to be heard via sound in the world, rather than imagined. A performer (or performers) making sounds with traditional or novel means is as acceptable as prepared sounds generated by a computer. The fact that we may refer as readily to instrumentalists "playing their instruments" as to someone hitting PLAY on a computer or other device sold me on the term, along with its added advantage of being conveniently translatable into many languages, and also its connotation of a pleasurable leisure activity that need not be anything more.

The pieces in this volume may be presented together as a collection, although this is not required. Individual pieces or a subset of pieces may also be presented, under their individual titles. When not presenting the full collection, explicit reference should be made to the overall work, *Playerbook*, either in program notes or parenthetically following individual titles (from *Playerbook*).

The durations of these works, though likely brief, may be any within reason, determined by the players, with the proviso that the chosen duration should primarily serve clarity in rendering the perceptual objectives of a given piece. One may opt for a longer duration, but not excessively longer than necessary to present it clearly.

Performers of *Playberbook* should be credited (in programs or liner notes) in such a way as *not* to imply that the work has prescribed their chosen sounding means—to emphasize that they are players of the piece first and foremost, and not instrumentalists, vocalists, etc. A general credit such as "player," "performer," or "members of the ensemble" is fine; any more specific listing—"computer," "piano," "voice," etc.—is not. Performer bios may refer to their specialization, but should avoid any implication that this is a requirement. To further the theater analogy, an actor playing a guest may choose to wear a red jacket, but would not be credited as "guest in red jacket" unless so dubbed by the playwright. The same character may change jackets or not wear one in subsequent performances, and the same goes for the sounding means chosen by players of *Playerbook*.

These pieces may be presented in-person or virtually (audio only or with video), with any or all sounds played in real-time or from a prepared source.

As with *Immaterial*, I am glad for Mark So's assistance in reading over these pieces to prevent indications that are more unwieldy than necessary.

Jason Thomas, 2024

Context Shifts (Sequential)

for anyone

Play a sound in isolation.

Pause.

Play the same sound, preceded by another subordinate sound which anticipates it.

Play the initial sound again in isolation.

Play a sound in isolation.

Pause.

Play the same sound, followed by another subordinate sound which reacts to it.

Play the initial sound again in isolation.

Context Shifts (Simultaneous)

for anyone

Play a sound in isolation.

Play the same sound along with one other simultaneously, such that the initial sound is primary.

Play the same sound along with one other simultaneously (different from previous), such that the initial sound is subordinate.

Play all three sounds simultaneously. Repeat a few times as desired, slightly varying the balance between the sounds each time.

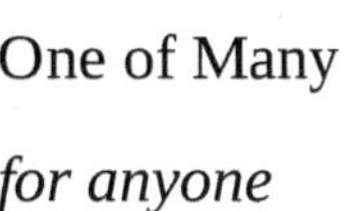

One of Many

for anyone

Play a single sound.

Play a series of sounds containing it, such that the sound played previously is not emphasized.

Embellishments

for anyone

Play a series of sounds or a single sound.

Play the same, with embellishments added.

Play the embellishment alone.

Sequiturs

for anyone

Play a series of sounds or a single sound.

Play the same, concluding with a different series or sound that follows logically.

Continue playing the initial series or sound, each time with a different consequent series or sound, as many times as desired. (This step is optional.)

Conclude by playing the series or sound as initially heard, without any consequent component.

Collections, Alone and Together

for anyone

Play two different collections of sounds, the second beginning prior to the conclusion of the first. Conclude the first collection while the second is underway.

Try to choose sounds that will have a synergistic effect through the middle period, during which the end of the first collection and beginning of second overlap, rather than treating the transition as a crossfade (one collection coming to the fore while the other recedes).

After a Pause

for anyone

Choose two sustaining sounds, slightly different from one another.

Play the first sound in full, followed by a pause, after which the second sound is played. Ensure the pause is long enough that the minor difference in sounds is not easily apparent, or does not command attention.

Play the same two sounds, with the latter immediately following the former, such that their minor difference is easily perceived.

Clarity and Obfuscation

for anyone

Play a series of sounds or a single sound.

Play again, obstructed or obfuscated by another simultaneous sound or series of sounds.

Play the second sound or series of sounds alone.

Interruptions

for anyone

Play a series of sounds.

Repeat with or without variation, once or perhaps more, depending on the sounds chosen.

Play another sound which interrupts this process, causing it to stop.

Play the original series and subsequent interruption as many times as desired (optional), depending on the variation available among the chosen sounds.

Accent and Other

for anyone

Play a sustaining sound that builds in some way and ends at the height of the build when accented by a second sound, such that they comprise a single statement.

Begin the same process again, this time increasing the starting and ending levels of the initial build, again ending with an accent from the other sound.

Repeat this process until the maximum level of the parameter is reached, with the final build ending abruptly at the upper limit, unaccented. Play the second sound as its own statement after a short pause, just long enough that the two sounds are now heard in succession as separate sonic events.

Individual and Group Contexts

for anyone

I

Play a single, simple sound comprising a single sonic element.

II

Play a series of sounds in sequence, each perceived as individual events.

Play the same sounds as a single sonic mass, with none exhibiting individual prominence.

III

Play a sustaining sound with a continuously evolving aspect which culminates as another sound accents it, such that this process comprises a single sonic event.

Play the evolving sound followed by the accenting sound after a slight pause, such that both are perceived as discrete sonic events.

Attention Drawn Elsewhere

for anyone

Play a series of sounds in a motor rhythm, such that no subdivisions or internal groupings are perceived.

While the initial series continues, play another series of sounds that gradually get farther apart rhythmically while their volume is gradually increased.

While both previous groups of sounds continue, play a series of sounds in erratic groupings of varying rhythm, at inconsistent or arbitrary volume levels between rhythmic groupings.

Relative Volume

for anyone

Play a steady sustaining sound that remains moderate in all aspects including volume and timbre, without variation.

While the previous sound continues, play a second brief sound at a higher volume.

Discontinue the initial sound shortly after the second sound ends.

Play the second sound alone, the same as before in every aspect except at a lower volume, such that the characteristics of the sound would not be perceived if played during the initial sound.

Accent Components

for anyone

Play several short decay sounds together as a compound accent at the start of a longer sustaining sound.

After the sustaining sound ends, play the accent sounds sequentially, with a brief pause between, so that each may be heard individually.

Play the long sustaining sound alone, without accent.

Pulse and Diversion

for anyone

Play the same sound two or more times, establishing a rhythmic pulse. (Same need not be interpreted literally, just materially similar, as perceived.)

After establishing the reiteration of the same, gradually change the sound until a more varied composite sequence of divergent sounds emerges, maintaining the same pulse.

Increase the variation of the sounds while gradually abandoning the singular rhythmic pulse so that eventually, the diverging component sounds share little or no rhythmic cohesion.

Increase the time between instances of each component sound and increase the variation within those component sounds as well, until there is no perceived coherence or coordination among the "parts."

Undulation and Accent

for anyone

Play a sustaining sound that undulates at a fairly steady rate.

After the sound has been established and a few undulations have occurred, accent the start of each undulation with a separate sound that has an immediate decay.

After a few accented undulations, the accenting sound cuts off the sustaining sound at the conclusion of an undulation. Play the accent sound a few more times, at the same interval between attacks as before (the duration of a full undulation), until this sound is perceived as primary, independent of the former sustaining sound.

Displacement

for anyone

Play a sequential group of sounds.

Play the same group, changing one sound only, such that it is displaced relative to the initial presentation of the group. While optional, no rhythmic pulse need be implied.

Stasis Points

for anyone

Play each of the following sonic elements, initially in isolation, then simultaneously:

A sound perceived as having pitch.

A sound comprising many repetitions of a sound, such that an overall texture is perceived.

Choose a duration just long enough to establish a uniform or static sonic texture that does not evolve over time. Avoiding prominent attack characteristics will help facilitate this objective.

Receding to Background

for anyone

Play a sustaining sound.

Having established and sustained the initial sound, play another sustaining sound while the first continues, such that the second sound becomes primary.

Boundaries and Increments

for anyone

Play a sound followed by the same sound, slightly different in some aspect.

Play the sound again, incrementally increasing the difference in the same sounding aspect over the course of a single iteration.

Continue this process a few times, each time increasing the difference in the same aspect.

Decreasing Boundaries

for anyone

Play a sound followed by the same sound, significantly altered in some aspect. (Take care to choose a feature that can be changed drastically while still maintaining the overall "sameness" of the sound.)

Continue this process a few times, decreasing the difference in the same aspect each time.

Stop either at a point you find aesthetically interesting, or when no perceived difference is left and two identical instances of the same sound are heard.

Clusters in Sequence

for anyone

Play a small number of sound groups in succession, each occupying a very narrow harmonic space. The component sounds may but need not be perceived as having pitch.

Duration and Timbre

for anyone

Play a long sustaining sound that is static in nature.

Shortly after this sound ends, play a sound of similar timbral quality, having a brief duration and immediate decay.

Individual and Group Versions

for anyone

Play a single sound. After a pause, play a different version of the same sound.

Pause briefly.

Play a series of sounds. After a pause, play a different version of the same series without changing any individual component sound.

Pause briefly.

Play a series of sounds. After a pause, play a different version of the same series which does change individual components.

Frenzy and Ritard

for anyone

Play a brief collection of sounds with no discernible order or rhythmic pattern.

Stop abruptly. After a brief pause, reiterate one sound repeatedly, gradually slowing. Continue until the time between iterations has increased such that sounds appear primarily as individuals rather than components of a slowing rhythmic pulse.

Obstruction and Coexistence

for anyone

Play two sustaining sounds simultaneously at a moderate volume, gradually increasing the volume of one until the other is obstructed.

After a brief pause, play the same two sustaining sounds at a moderate volume again, gradually increasing the volume of the previously obstructed sound until it obstructs the other.

After a brief pause, play the same two sustaining sounds at a moderate volume, remaining in equal balance such that both are clear and unobstructed.

Exposure and Suppression (Gradual)

for anyone

Play a repeating rhythmic pulse on a clear, consistent sound.

Gradually suppress the sound over time. (This may be done in a variety of ways, but not exclusively through lowered volume.)

Exposure and Suppression (Immediate)

for anyone

Play a repeating rhythmic pulse on a clear, consistent sound.

At some point after establishing the pulse, suppress the sound. (This may be done in a variety of ways, but not exclusively through lowered volume.)

Increments and Categories

for anyone

Play a series of sounds, incrementally different in some way.

Play a series of sounds, categorically different from the first.

Alternating Changes

for anyone

Choose two different sounds that can incrementally change in some way, though not necessarily in the same way.

Play the sounds in repeated alternation, each changing incrementally with each iteration such that two alternating changes are perceived.

Continuity and Conclusion

for anyone

Choose any previously played piece or portion of a piece from this collection and play it in such a way that it appears conclusive. While the player can make use of the same interpretive liberty implicit when playing the piece before, it should be recognizable as the same piece (or portion thereof) reinterpreted and recontextualized, rather than a different piece entirely.

www.ingramcontent.com/pod-product-compliance
Lightning Source LLC
LaVergne TN
LVHW061258100826
845148LV00008B/1167